THE COMPLETE SAXOPHONE PLAYER
BOOK 2
by Raphael Ravenscroft.

Wise Publications
London / New York / Sydney

Exclusive Distributors:

Music Sales Limited
8/9 Frith Street, London W1V 5TZ, England.

Music Sales Corporation
225 Park Avenue South, New York, NY 10003, USA.

Music Sales Pty. Limited
120 Rothschild Avenue, Rosebery, NSW 2018, Australia.

This book © Copyright 1987 by
Wise Publications
ISBN 0.7119.0888.5
Order No. AM 62720

Book designed by Sands Straker.
Cover designed by Pearce Marchbank.
Engraved by Music Print.
Typeset by Capital Setters.

Music Sales complete catalogue lists thousands of titles
and is free from your local music book shop, or direct
from Music Sales Limited.
Please send a cheque or postal order for £1.50 for postage to
Music Sales Limited, 8/9 Frith Street, London W1V 5TZ, England.

Printed in England by
Halstan & Co. Limited, Amersham, Bucks.

Contents

Welcome To Book Two

You have covered a lot of ground since you first opened *Book One* of *The Complete Saxophone Player* and it is my aim to help you to continue to move on rapidly to becoming The Complete Saxophone Player.

In *Book Two* you will learn more about *new notes* and *fingerings*. Discover all about *tuning* and *intonation, scales* and *riff patterns,* and see how *rhythm* relates to *different playing styles.* All the Sessions are *graded,* each introducing one of *twenty-seven* popular tunes.

You will not find anything difficult in this book as long as you have successfully completed *Book One.* If you are working on your own, don't forget to keep practising regularly every day.

Remember: This series is based on popular songs, with easy-to-follow text and clear diagrams. *The Complete Saxophone Player* will *show* you, rather than *lecture, encourage* you, rather than *demand* from you, and always keep you progressing rapidly. So, enjoy the instrument in your own time at your own pace.

Have Fun . . .

The Saxophone's 'Top Ten'

Listening to other saxophone players is one of the best ways of improving your playing style and tone. Try to analyse what you hear, listen to the phrasing and if possible get recordings of the same tune played by different artists. In this way you will discover how a melody can be 'interpreted' in many ways.

To get some idea of what the saxophone is capable of, try to listen to recordings by as many of these artists as possible. There are many other fine players of course, but these are my 'Top Ten' (in alphabetical order):

Michael Brecker
Ornette Coleman
Stan Getz
Johnnie Hodges
Charlie Parker
Dave Sanborn
Tom Scott
Grover Washington
Ben Webster
Phil Woods

What You Have Achieved So Far

Don't forget the following points from *Book One:*

1. Instrument Assembly

Reed, mouthpiece and ligature assembly. Crook
and mouthpiece assembly. Main instrument
assembly.

2. Playing Position

Correct posture. Correct finger placements.
Comfortable embouchure.

3. Breathing Technique

Diaphragmatic breathing. Diaphragmatic support.

4. Music Theory

Pitch notation. Key signatures. Rhythmic notation.
Time signatures. Notes: D to C.

Dotted notes
Sharp, flat, and natural signs

5. General Techniques

Tonguing. Playing legato. Octave key technique.

You will find *Book One* a handy reference.

Session One: Bars with Two Beats and Tuning Procedures

Let's get straight back into playing with the Paul Simon classic 'The Sound of Silence'.

Bar 9 has only *two* beats. See how this is written in music notation.

The Sound Of Silence
Words & Music by Paul Simon

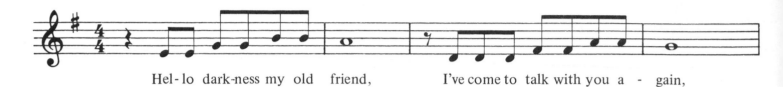

Hel - lo dark-ness my old friend, I've come to talk with you a - gain,

be-cause a vis - ion soft - ly creep - ing left its seeds while I was sleep - ing,

and the vi - sion that was plan - ted in my brain still re -

mains with - in the sound of si - lence.

In rest - less dreams I walked a - lone nar - row streets of cob - ble - stone,

'neath the ha - lo of a street lamp, ___ I turned my col-lar to the cold and damp ___

when my eyes were stabbed by the flash of a ne - on light that split the

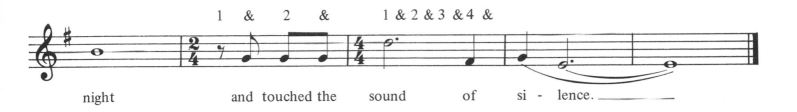

night and touched the sound of si - lence. _____

Tuning Up

Should you not have the use of a piano, invest in a tuning fork from your local music store. Alternatively, if you have a battery operated metronome it will almost certainly put out an electronic 'beep'. This will probably be the note A = 440 Hertz. This is fingered as F sharp on alto and baritone sax, or B natural on tenor and soprano sax.

Tuning the saxophone is a subtle process and is to do with very small changes in pitch. These changes vary according to the depth to which the mouthpiece is pushed on to the crook.

Poor intonation (playing out of tune) is one of the most common faults found in saxophone students.

Tuning up should become an integral part of your playing routine and will help to develop aural awareness and tone quality, because good sound and good intonation are inseparable. If, at any time in your practice sessions, your playing sounds out of tune, stop and go through the tuning method.

Tuning Method

Using the piano/tuning fork/metronome as reference, adjust the *mouthpiece* so that the corresponding note is as near to the given note as possible. Start off with your normal embouchure, and by relaxing or tightening the lower jaw slightly, you will notice a slight variation in pitch. This movement should enable you to hear the difference in pitch relative to the given note. Now, ask yourself these questions:

1. When I loosen or tighten up, am I getting closer to matching the pitch or further away from it?
2. Does my embouchure still feel comfortable, or does it feel tense and pinched?

If you find that the note you are producing is *sharp* (higher) relative to the given tone, pull the mouthpiece *out* a little. Conversely, if the note seems too *flat* (lower) relative to the given tone, push the mouthpiece further on to the crook.

Golden Rule:
Never pinch to get the pitch.

Session Two: The Repeat Sign

This session introduces you to a new musical sign –
the *repeat sign*. This means that you repeat all the
music between these two signs – *once.*

When the repeat is back to the beginning of a piece
the first repeat sign can be omitted.

As you can see, this song contains two repeated
sections.

Ob-La-Di, Ob-La-Da
Words & Music by John Lennon & Paul McCartney

♩ = 200

Des-mond has a   bar- row in the mar- ket   place ___   Mol - ly   is   the

sing - er   in the   band _____   Des-mond says to Mol - ly, girl I

like your   face ___ and Mol - ly   says this as   she takes him by   the   hand. ___

___   Ob - la — di   ob - la — da   life goes   on _____   bra,

la la how the life goes on. _____ In a cou-ple of

years they have built a home sweet home.

With a couple of kids run-ning in the yard of

Des-mond and Mol-ly Jones. Hap-py ev-er af-ter in the

mar-ket place ____ Des-mond lets the child-ren lend a hand ____

Mol-ly stays at home and does her pret-ty face____ and in the eve-ning she still

sings it with the band. _____ Ob — la — di ob — la — da, life goes

Repeat and Fade

on _____ bra la la how the life goes on. ____

Session Three: First And Second Time Bars

Some pieces contain *first* and *second time* bars in addition to the repeat signs.

They look – and work – like this:

After making repeat
omit this bar and go to 2.

These two popular songs contain an example of first and second time bars.

Arrivederci Roma

Words by Garinei & Giovannini English Lyrics by Carl Sigma
Music by Renato Rascel

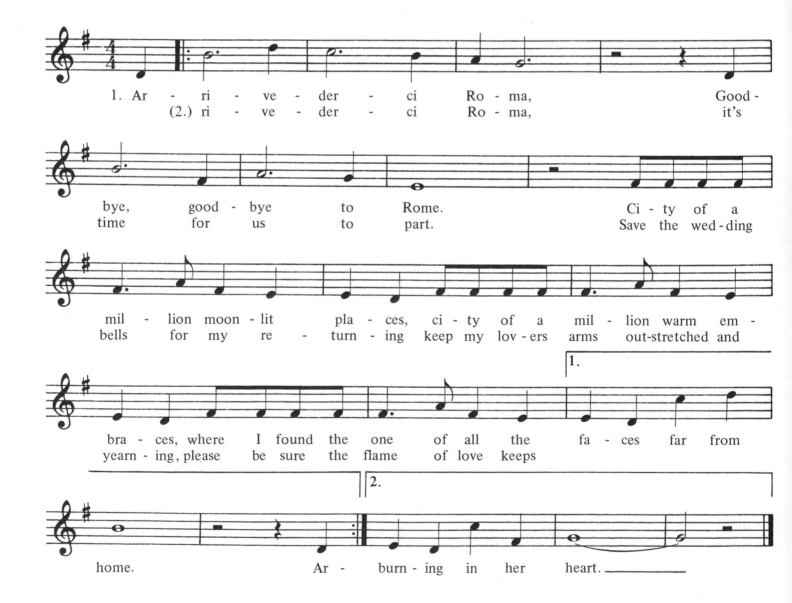

1. Ar - ri - ve - der - ci Ro - ma,   Good -
(2.) ri - ve - der - ci Ro - ma,   it's

bye,   good - bye   to   Rome.   Ci - ty of a
time   for   us   to   part.   Save the wed - ding

mil - lion moon - lit   pla - ces, ci - ty of a mil - lion warm em -
bells   for   my   re - turn - ing keep my lov - ers arms   out-stretched and

bra - ces, where I found the one of all the   fa - ces far from
yearn - ing, please be sure the flame of love keeps

home.   Ar - burn - ing in her heart. _____

All My Loving

Words & Music by John Lennon & Paul McCartney

Brightly

1. Close your eyes and I'll kiss you To - mor - row I'll
2. - tend that I'm kiss - ing The lips I am

miss you; Re - mem - ber I'll al - ways be true. _____ And then
miss - ing And hope that my dreams will come true. _____

while I'm a - way, I'll write home ev - 'ry day, _____ And I'll

1.

send all my lov - ing to you. _____ I'll pre -

2.

_____ All my lov - ing I will send to you. _____

_____ All my lov - ing, dar - ling, I'll be true. _____

Session Four: Scales Or Scale-Riffs

Let's learn our first scale. I prefer to call it scale-riff.
As you are about to discover, you have already
played this scale in a slightly different form in
Book One.

The scale of G Major.

Now let's play another tune using sections of this
scale.

Hello Little Girl
Words & Music by John Lennon & Paul McCartney

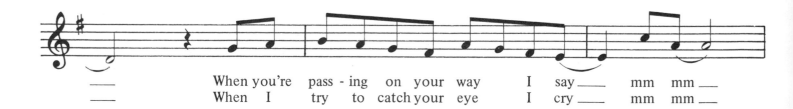

1. When I see you ev - 'ry day I say ___ mm mm ___ Hel - lo ___ lit - tle girl.
2.   see you pass-ing by I cry ___ mm mm ___ Hel - lo ___ lit - tle girl.

___ When you're pass - ing on your way I say ___ mm mm ___
___ When I try to catch your eye I cry ___ mm mm ___

Hel - lo ___ lit - tle girl. ___ If I
Hel - lo ___ lit - tle girl. _ ___ I send you flow - ers but

you don't care, ___ you nev - er seem to see me stand - ing there. ___

I of - ten won - der what you're think-ing of ___ I hope it's me, love, love love. ___ So I hope there'll come a day when you'll say ___ mm mm ___ you're my ___ lit - tle girl, ___ you're my ___ lit - tle girl ___

You will notice that the tune consists *only* of the notes of the G Major scale arranged rhythmically in such a way that the ear hears them as a series of *tensions* and *resolutions* (discussed in Book One). These *tensions* and *resolutions* are the focal points of any good tune or improvised solo, as we shall learn later.

Here is another example

The Ballad Of Davy Crockett
Words by Tom Blackburn   Music by George Bruns

Session Five: Technical Exercises

While playing the scale of G Major you may have noticed that the note change: B to C and C to D is not as fluent as some of the other note changes.

This is due not only to the design of the instrument, but also because certain finger movements are easier than others.

Play the following passage until you are satisfied with the smoothness of your fingering.

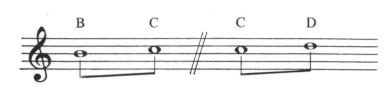

While playing the next tune, concentrate on the note changes B to C and C to D.

The Sound Of Music

Words by Oscar Hammerstein II   Music by Richard Rodgers

Moderately

The hills are a-live with the sound of mu - sic _____ with

songs they have sung for a thou - sand years _____ the

hills fill my heart with the sound of mu - sic, _____ my

heart wants to sing ev-'ry song it hears. _____

Session Six: The Warm-Up

Play the following examples slowly at first and then increase the speed until you are able to slur or articulate each passage at a fairly bright tempo.

Remember:
The tongue must be used to cleanly articulate those notes not written under a slur. All the other notes should be played evenly with no tongue articulation.

These passages will help you to co-ordinate fingers and tongue and, in so doing, prepare you for the next songs.

Kum Ba Yah

Folk Song

Love's Been Good To Me

Words & Music by Rod McKuen

Moderately

I have been a ro - ver   I have walked a - lone,

hiked a hun - dred high - ways   nev - er found a home.

Still in all I'm hap - py   the rea - son is you see

once in a while a - long the way,   love's been good to me. There was a

girl in Den - ver   be - fore the sum - mer storm

oh her arms were ten - der   oh, her arms were warm, and she could

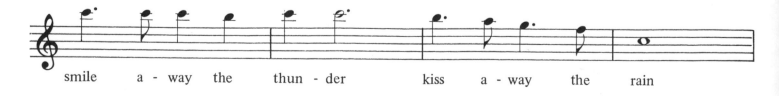

smile a - way the thun - der   kiss a - way the rain

16

and ev - en though she's gone a - way you won't hear me com - plain.

I have been a ro - ver I have walked a - lone

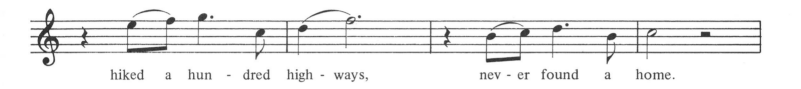

hiked a hun - dred high - ways, nev - er found a home.

Still in all I'm hap - py the rea - son is you see

*This sign means hold note.

once in a while a - long the way, love's been good to me.

* When playing with a band or orchestra the conductor will direct how long a pause note (marked ⌢) should be held. In the absence of such direction the player should hold the note for the amount of time that feels correct.

Session Seven: Long Notes

The importance of producing a full, evenly supported sound, becomes apparent when you are called on to play tunes with *long notes*. In this next tune, try to organise your sound production in such a way that it does not become faint and 'wobbly' when holding the long notes.

Remember:
To produce a full, rounded tone you should concentrate on keeping a relaxed throat/embouchure and a tight supportive diaphragm (refer to session on breathing, Book One, p.13).

Sailing
Words & Music by Gavin Sutherland

I am sail - ing I am sail - ing home a - gain ___ 'cross the sea I am

sail - ing storm - y wa - ters to be near ___ you to be free I am

fly - ing I am fly - ing like a bird ___ 'cross the sky I am

fly - ing pass - ing high clouds to be with ___ you to be free.

Session Eight: Dynamic Indications (Loud And Soft)

The use of dynamics is one of the most important aspects of music. Listen to any great soloist and it won't be long before you hear what I mean. Dynamics are a very important part of any good solo, so let's look into this area with *your* own future solos in mind.

Traditionally, musical dynamics are written in Italian! Fortunately there are not many in everyday use so familiarise yourself with this short list.

Dynamics

Fortissimo	Very loud	*ff*
Forte	Loud	*f*
Mezzo-forte	Medium-loud	*mf*
Mezzo-piano	Medium-soft	*mp*
Piano	Soft	*p*
Pianissimo	Very Soft	*pp*
Getting louder		
Getting softer		

Now play these examples which illustrate the use of dynamics.

The following piece contains many examples of musical dynamics.

William Tell Overture

By Gioacchino Rossini

Session Nine: New Note – 'Bottom C'

For the note Bottom C place your right-hand little finger (R4) over the key R42 (lower of the two possible keys).

When you start playing notes as low as this, good *support* is essential. Also, I would suggest you start at a higher note, (say G), and work downwards by step in order to avoid the *'honking'* syndrome.

The Note C (B♯)

Bottom C

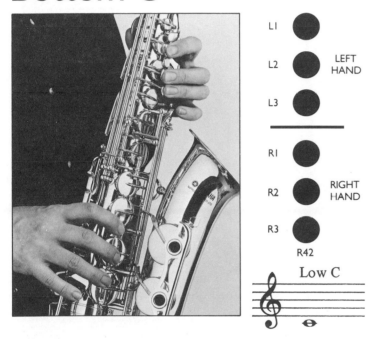

```
L1    ●
L2    ●    LEFT
           HAND
L3    ●
─────────────
R1    ●
R2    ●    RIGHT
           HAND
R3    ●
R42
```

Low C

Learning this note enables us to extend our knowledge of scales to include C Major which is written like this:

Now let's try a tune in C Major.

Spanish Harlem

Words & Music by Jerry Leiber & Phil Spector

Moderate - Latin feel

There is a rose in Span-ish Har-lem

a rare rose up in Span-ish Har-lem.

It is a spec - ial one it's nev - er seen the sun, it on - ly

comes up when the moon is on the run and all the stars are gleam-ing.

1. It's grow-ing in the street right up thro' the con - crete but

soft and sound in pale noon.

2. I'm going to pick that rose and watch her as she grows __

__ in my gar - den.

Session Ten: Preparation for Playing New Tunes

It is often easier to *sing* a new tune before playing it. Why not try singing or whistling this popular tune before attempting it on your saxophone.

Sunny
Words & Music by Bobby Hebb

Session Eleven: Pitching

Let's try another tune. Listen to the intervals *between* different pitches, always ensuring they are the same. Remember to use your lower jaw to correct any tuning discrepancy.

Feelings

English Words & Music by Morris Albert
Spanish Lyric by Thomas Fundora

Slow - ballad feel

Feel - ings ___ noth-ing more than feel - ings ___ try - ing to for -

- get my feel - ings of love. get my ___

feel - ings of love. Feel - ings ___ for all my life I'll

feel it I wish I'd nev - er met you girl you nev-er come a - gain.

Feel - ings, wo wo wo feel - ings wo wo wo

feel   you   a - gain in my   arms.   Feel - ings ___

feel - ings like I've nev - er lost you   and feel-ings like I'll nev - er have_ you

a - gain in my   heart.   arms.

We often see the letters D.C. & D.S. in a piece of music. D.C. (from the Italian *da capo*) tells us to return to the beginning ('top'). D.S. (*dal segno*) means return to the sign, 𝄋 . After these letters we see the words *al coda* (to the *coda*).

The *coda* is the end section of a song, usually short. Here is an example:

Here we play bars 1–3. We are then directed back to bar 2 (𝄋), and continue to bar 3, when the sign above the bar line tells us to jump to the *coda* at bar 4.

Session Twelve: New Time Signatures

Although I mentioned this time signature in Book One, I did not explain its musical relevance.

In the example below you will notice that the bar in 6/8 time appears to be divided into two halves. This is because music written in this time signature has a *two beat* overall pulse structure, i.e. instead of the four main pulses of a bar of 4/4, the 6/8 bar has two main pulses, each of which is divided into three sub-pulses.

A bar of $\frac{4}{4}$ contains 8 quavers grouped like this:

A bar of $\frac{6}{8}$ contains 6 quavers grouped like this:

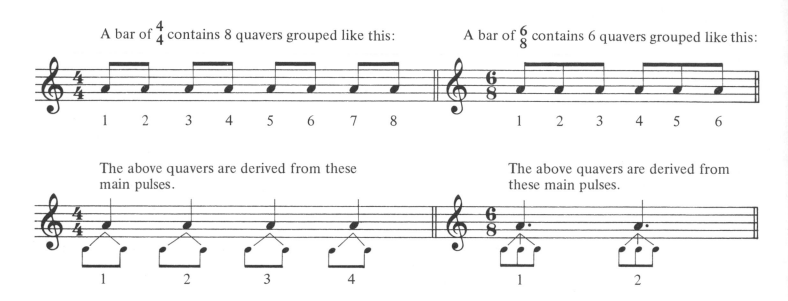

The above quavers are derived from these main pulses.

The above quavers are derived from these main pulses.

The following example uses the time signature 6/8.

Morning Has Broken

Words by Eleanor Farjeon. Music by Cat Stevens

Moderate

mf Morn-ing has bro - ken, like the first morn - ing black bird has spo - ken

like the first bird _____ praise for the sing - ing praise for the morn -

ing praise for them spring - ing, fresh from the world. Sweet the rains

new fall, sun lit from hea - ven, like the first dew fall

on the first grass._____ Praise for the sweet - ness of the wet gar -

den, sprung in com - plete - ness, where his feet pass. Morn - ing has

bro - ken like the first morn - ing, black bird has spo - ken

like the first bird _____ praise for the sing - ing praise for the morn -

ing praise for them spring - ing fresh from the world. _____

Session Thirteen: Rhythmic Exercises

I have no doubt that your ability to read difficult rhythms is developing rapidly. So, at this point, we shall take time to consolidate what you have learned so far.

Put your instrument down and clap through the following series of rhythmic exercises.

Rhythm is very important in Latin American music.
Try playing this 'Latin Standard' taking special care
with the articulation.

La Cucaracha
Traditional

Session Fourteen: Solos

Now, let's play another well known solo, remembering to concentrate on the *rhythm*. If you are having difficulties refer to the previous session.

Careless Whisper
Words & Music by George Michael & Andrew Ridgeley

Here is that well known extract from Billy Joel's hit *'Just The Way You Are'*. The track can be found on the album *'The Stranger'* and the sax soloist is Phil Woods.

Just The Way You Are
Words & Music by Billy Joel

Play this tune, again concentrating on the
rhythm.

I'd Like To Teach The World To Sing

Words & Music by Roger Cook, Roger Greenaway,
Billy Backer & Billy Davis

I'd like to build the world a home — and fur - nish it with

love grow ap - ple trees and hon - ey bees and snow white tur - tle

doves I'd like to teach the world — to sing — in per - fect har - mo - ny —

— I'd like to hold it in my arms and keep it com - pa - ny. —

— I'd like to see the world — for once all stand - ing hand in hand

— and hear them ech - o through — the hills for peace through - out the land.

That's the song I hear __ let the world sing to - day, a
song of peace that ech- oes on __ and nev - er goes a - way. __ I'd
like to build the world a home __ and fur - nish it with love grow
ap - ple trees and hon - ey bees and snow-white tur - tle doves. I'd
like to teach the world __ to sing __ in per - fect har - mo - ny __ I'd
like to hold it in my arms and keep it com - pa - ny. __ I'd
like to see the world __ for once all stand-ing hand in hand __ and
hear them ech - o through __ the hills for peace through-out the land. __

Session Fifteen: New Notes B♭ and E♭ And New Scales

Now, let's learn two new notes:
B flat and E flat.

B Flat (A♯) is written and fingered like this:

E Flat (D♯) is written and fingered like this:

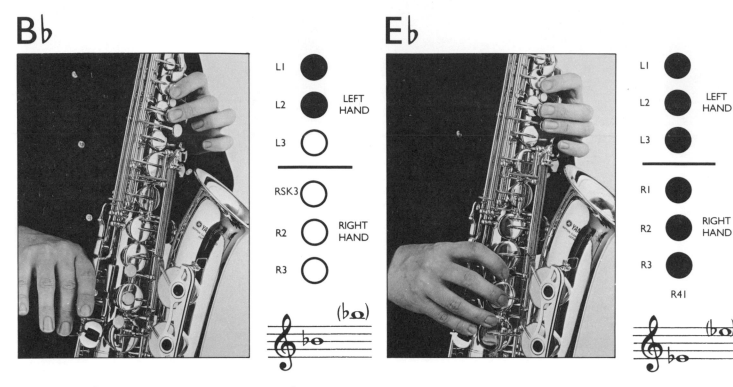

Learning these two major notes expands your scale capabilities to include two new Major scales. F major and B flat major.

Scale of F Major:

Scale of B flat Major:

Session Sixteen: Using the Scale of Fmajor

Earlier in the book you played this song in the key of *G Major.* Now let's try the same piece using the notes of the scale of *F Major.*

All My Loving
Words & Music by John Lennon & Paul McCartney

f Close your eyes and I'll kiss you to - mor - row I'll miss you re - mem - ber I'll

al - ways be true _____ and then while I'm a - way I'll write

home ev - 'ry day ____ And I'll send all my lov - ing to you. ____

____ All my lov - ing, I will send to you, _____ all my

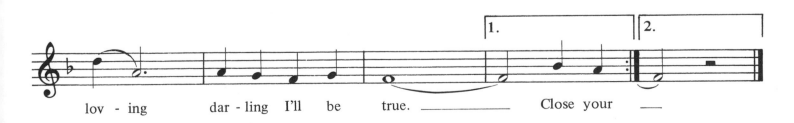

lov - ing dar - ling I'll be true. _____ Close your ____

Session Seventeen: The Key of BFlat Major

This song is in the key of B flat Major which has two flats (B flat and E flat). Watch out for the accidental in bar twelve.

Killing Me Softly With His Song
Words by Norman Gimbel. Music by Charles Fox

Slow - ballad

I heard he sang ___ a good song I ___ heard he

had a style ___ and so I came ___ to see him and

list - en for ___ a while ___ and there ___ he was ___ this young_ boy

a stran - ger to my eyes, _____ strum-ming my pain with his fin -

- gers _____ sing - ing my life ___ with his words _____

kill-ing me soft - ly with his ___ song kill-ing me soft - ly ___ with his ___

___ song tell-ing my whole ___ life ___ with his ___ words kill-ing me soft -

- ly ___ with his song. ___

The first section of the verse of this well known
tune incorporates B flats and B natural, also
watch out for the F sharp accidentals.

Sunrise Sunset

Words by Sheldon Harnick   Music by Jerry Bock

Slow waltz time

Session Eighteen: Triplets

We have already encountered a form of the *triplet* in the chapter dealing with 6/8 time. Do you remember how I referred to the *two* main pulses divided into *three* 'sub pulses' (three quavers).

A bar of $\frac{6}{8}$ contains 6 quavers grouped like this:

With songs written in 4/4 or 2/4 time the underlying pulse structure is two quavers (eighth notes) for each crotchet (quarter note). If we wish to introduce variety, we can write and play *three* quavers in the time normally taken to play two. This is called a *triplet*. Let me demonstrate this to you musically.

The above quavers are derived from these main pulses:

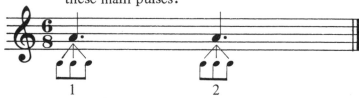

This is the most common subdivision of the crotchet (quarter note) pulse.

Quavers

However, we can also sub-divide each crotchet into triplets (3 equal parts).

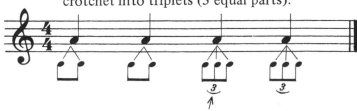

This figure indicates that the crotchet is divided into three equal parts.

This tune is a very good introduction to quaver triplets. There is a two beat introduction (called a 'pick up') before the double bar line so count a silent first beat before you play the first group of triplets.

It's All In The Game

Music by Charles G. Dawes   Words by Carl Sigman

Session Nineteen: Practice Suggestions

By now you will be well on the way to developing your own personal sound. Always remember the importance of *tone quality,* it is a major factor in performances. Your tone quality is easily improved by playing long notes *correctly* i.e. with good posture, even breathing and the simple but effective habit of blowing warm, rather than cold air into the instrument.

Let's play a song from the Rock Opera 'Superstar' by Tim Rice and Andrew Lloyd Webber.

I Don't Know How To Love Him

Music by Andrew Lloyd Webber   Lyrics by Tim Rice

Listen carefully to the pitch of your notes. If possible try playing, even practising, with more experienced players. Listen to their pitch and sound and try to match it.

Hints: To develop good intonation, align your pitch with a piano. Always be sure when playing with a recorded accompaniment that the record or tape is in tune. ('A' 440 Hertz). I have found that recording parts of my practice sessions makes me more critically aware of the weaker points in my playing.

Also, *recording* your playing is the only way you can hear exactly how you sound.

The *crotchet triplets* you will encounter in this piece should be approached in the same way as the quaver triplets you encountered in Book Two.
A *quaver triplet* is a crotchet divided into three equal parts and a *crotchet triplet* is a minim divided into three equal parts.

Theme from 'EastEnders'
Composed by Leslie Osborne & Simon May

New Notes: C# and Low C#

By now you will have arrived at the point where you should be expanding your horizons with new notes, so let's add a few to your repertoire.

Firstly: C♯ (D♭) is written and fingered like this:

C♯

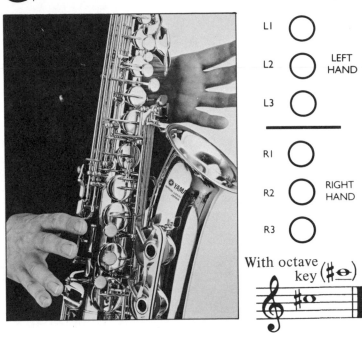

L1 ⃝	
L2 ⃝	LEFT HAND
L3 ⃝	
─────────	
R1 ⃝	
R2 ⃝	RIGHT HAND
R3 ⃝	

With octave key (♯𝅝)

In the lowest octave, the C♯ is slightly more involved. Take a close look at this chart and ensure you have the correct finger positions.

Low C♯

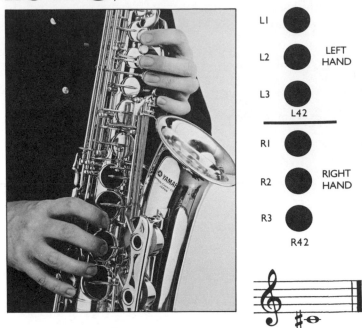

L1 ●	
L2 ●	LEFT HAND
L3 ●	
──L42──	
R1 ●	
R2 ●	RIGHT HAND
R3 ●	
R42	

Having learned the note C♯, we are able to play the *D major* scale. Let's try it.

Hint: Run up and down this scale a few times (without blowing). This allows you to concentrate on the finger positions.

Here's a well known big-band favourite in the key of
G Major.

American Patrol
Composed by F.W. Meacham

The next song is one of my favourites and is a classic
from the jazz repertoire. Notice how I have written
it in the key of D Major.

Perfidia

English Lyric by Milton Leeds
Music & Spanish Words by Alberto Dominguez

The final tune you are going to play in Book Two is
the beautiful ballad by Chris de Burgh – 'The Lady
In Red'. The song has quite a few 'gaps' in the
melody line. Remember to keep counting through
the bars of silence.

The Lady In Red

Words & Music by Chris de Burgh

___ that catch _ your eyes, ___ I have _ been blind.__ The_
___ and ut - ter love, ___ as I do _ to - night.___

la - dy in red _____ is danc - ing __ with __

__ me, cheek to cheek, __ there's no - bo - dy here, __

__ it's just you and me, __

it's where I wan-na be, but I hard-ly know _____

this beau - ty by my side, _____ I'll

1.

nev - er for - get the way you look _ to - night._

46

(Instrumental)

2. I've   way you look — to-night, —

I   nev-er will — for - get ———   the   way   you

look   to - night. ——   The   la - dy   in   red,

my   la - dy   in   red.

I will briefly highlight the areas covered in this book, and then close with a scale chart which includes all the scales learnt in Books One and Two.

Firstly, by way of a reminder, we discussed:
1. Tunes with different length bars.
2. Suggestions for smooth playing (Legato – Italian musical term).
3. Repeat signs, First and Second Time bars.
4. Warm-up exercises.
5. Long notes and tone quality.
6. Dynamics.
7. New notes (Low C, B flat and E flat).
8. New scales.
9. Tuning up.
10. 6/8 time signature.
11. Triplets.

New notes (low C and C sharp, B flat, E flat and low C sharp)

C major

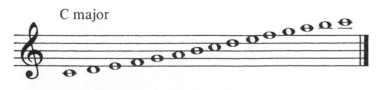

G major

F major

B♭ major

D major

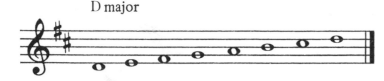

Have fun with your new skills and show off to your friends.

See you in Book Three!